mund Huber

Blind Huber

poems by

NICK FLYNN

Graywolf Press
Saint Paul, Minnesota

Publication of this volume is made possible in part by a grant provided by the Minnesota State Arts Board, through an appropriation by the Minnesota State Legislature, a grant from the Wells Fargo Foundation Minnesota, and a grant from the National Endowment for the Arts. Significant support has also been provided by the Bush Foundation; Marshall Field's Project Imagine with support from the Target Foundation; the McKnight Foundation; and other generous contributions from foundations, corporations, and individuals. To these organizations and individuals we offer our heartfelt thanks.

Special funding for this title has been provided by the Jerome Foundation.

Published by Graywolf Press
2402 University Avenue, Suite 203
Saint Paul, MN 55114
All rights reserved.

www.graywolfpress.org

Published in the United States of America

ISBN: 1-55597-373-6

2 4 6 8 9 7 5 3 1
First Graywolf Printing, 2002

Library of Congress Control Number: 2002102973

Cover photograph: Morgan Mazzoni,
Africanized killer bee's tail end (Apis mellifera scutellata)
© Tony Stone

Cover design: Scott Sorenson

extracts

for F.R.

He already had the water, but he had to discover jars . . .

—Thich Nhat Hanh, *The Heart of Buddhist Teaching*

Blind Huber (i)

Opaque glow where my eyes should be,

what remaining light, eyelids

thin against it. Soothing,

as if all I pass were encrusted in wax,

dipped upright—wax bush & wax

bench, wax man, wax tea, waxy cup to waxy

lips, my eyes now more like their eyes,

morning filtered beyond translucence

as the acolytes cover their queen.

By the sound they will soon

swarm, clockwork, the frenzied heat of wings

forms droplets on the walls of

their city, their city softening, now twisting

just out of shape.

Swarm

When you see us swarm—rustle of

wingbeat, collapsed air—your mind
tries to make us one, a common

intelligence, a single spirit un-
tethered. You imagine us merely
searching out the next

vessel, anything

that could contain us, as if the hive
were just another jar. You try

to hold the ending, this
unspooling, make it either

zero or many, lack

or flurry. *I was born,*
you begin, & already each word
makes you smaller. Look at this field—

Cosmos. Lungwort. Utter each
& break

into a thousand versions of yourself.

You can't tell your stories fast enough.
The answer is not one, but also

not two.

Blind Huber (ii)

I sit in a body & think of a body, I picture

Burnens' hands, my words

make them move. I say, *plunge them into the hive,*

& his hands go in. If I said,

put your head inside,

he would wear it. Think of my body, every day

the same chair, angled

thus, Burnens

every day, think of his body, think of

a hive, each bee, each thought, the hive

brims with thought. *Move it into shade,* I think,

& the body moves to shade. Whose

fingers, which word, each surges

from inside my head, but always returns

as Burnens.

Workers (attendants)

Nights we lie beside her, our mouths
at her belly, counting

her breaths, the buzz, the gathering, long
done. We all began
inside her, like those lined up

inside her now, mere
idea of ourselves
unborn. We wash her body

ceaselessly, move our tongues
until all her hairs loosen. She

roams the brood, finds
another empty cell

& fills it. Morning comes &
she calms us, keeps us inside
until the dew burns off. This sodden

world. All winter

we huddled around her, kept her
warm. Those on the outside, those
farthest from her, died

first, their legs
gripped the others like a shawl.

Hive

What would you do inside me?
You would be utterly

lost, labyrinthine

comb, each corridor identical, a
funhouse, *there,* a bridge, worker

knit to worker, a span
you can't cross. On the other side

the queen, a fortune of honey.

Once we filled an entire house with it,
built the comb between floorboard

& joist, slowly at first, the constant

buzz kept the owners awake, then
louder, until honey began to seep

from the walls, swell
the doorframes. Our gift.

They had to burn the house down
to rid us.

Blind Huber (iii)

Sometimes bees, the glittering

curtain they form, cling to my face,

& the moment before knowing

I can imagine them a leaf, able to be

brushed away, but they

hold on, their tongues

seek each pore,

as if my cheek offered nectar, they move

delicately, caress &

shade, as if not threatening

to flood my eyes.

Queen

Net suit &
smoking cup, you reek fear.
If we fight back, or if there isn't

enough, you seek me out with gloved fingers
to crush my head. When we sting

you scream. We know why

you carry our white boxes
to the edge of the alfalfa, to the figs

& raspberries. You take our honey
because we let you. We pollinate the fields

because we are the fields.

Workers (guards)

At night skunks come,

crack us in their teeth, oblivious
to the sting. We covered one

& its body jumped & we each died

pumping it with venom. The virgin
flew this morning
as we dragged the old queen

out. A drone

failed to follow, a young one,
gorging himself on honey,

& ten of us surrounded him,
held his mouth shut. We are

infinitely more abundant
& we are all the same.

Blind Huber (iv)

False kingdom, even as a child I knew—

no endpoint, no start—first

the hive creates a queen, so the queen

can create workers, so the workers can

build the hive. I tell Burnens, *seal it,*

& he seals it, presses his

fist to the opening, becomes

their cage. If the sun breaks through

they will find a way out, made

desperate by the hint of distant nectar,

tear a hole like a thought in their wall.

Virgin Queen

Utterly desired, translucent
body, wings

never tried, wax-sealed until
ready. The nurses feed me from their own
mouths

& I am changed,
made essential. They guard me
with their lives. Around us

comb spirals out, first

the lesser eggs, then stores
of pollen, honey pockets. I hear

a roar, an enormous wind,
twenty thousand

fanning my nectar. I'll gnaw my
way out, soon, smell

 17

where the other virgins sleep,
trapped

in that perfection forever.

Drones

We are made of waiting—

attendants tend the queen, nurses
nurse the grubs, we roam
the brood, sicken ourselves on honey

we did nothing to produce. Foragers
return with more, we rub against

their sexless bodies, taste
where they've been, this outside

coming in. A virgin grows in a guarded
cell, ripening on
rare jelly, we wait for her

to emerge. First she will kill

the other virgins, those
unborn, a spike

to the head, then lead us into a cloud

& fuck us in the air. Spacious
inside her, the root breaks off
to pump forever there. We

wait. The workers—
they would smother us all

if not for her.

Twinned

To exist wholly in another, seamless,
mirrored. Think of the hive,

at each turn we find ourselves, not
a version, not a replica,
but our whole selves. *Love,*

you claim, comes close to this,
no space

between your words, a hand

over the other's heart. How do you live
with this distance? *I have you,* she
thinks, or, *I know you,*

but she can never say, *I am you.*

Blind Huber (v)

Before shadows I saw the rose,

                    saw its thorn,

a bee navigating, never impaled.

I no longer know what is outside my mind

& what is in.

It must be the sun . . . there wasn't anything here but the sun in the first place . . . earth came out of the sun, and we came out of the earth . . .

—Major Amberson, *The Magnificent Ambersons,* upon dying

Inside Nothing

A sun-fed engine, the inside

constant, a flower taken
whole. In winter our wings

move faster, to keep the sun
inside, inside nothing

& we fill the nothing with suns,

line them up,
swallow sap, swallow

field, drop by drop, each stem
a pump. Rose to rose to rose to
rose to rose to rose to rose, calyx &

anther, all summer

gone. We move
still faster, fields grow

constant, inside
the color of heat. Clinging we
pull our bodies

across a chain of bodies, become

the chain, climb nothing,
always
up, toward suns, line them up

inside us, a flower taken whole,

a field built inside. It rises.
Each blade, each sun.

Blind Huber (vi)

Our words mingle &

entwine, I say, *ambrosia,*

he says, *night,* the visible world &

the invisible, who speaks by now

unimportant. Honey, you imagine,

must fall like rain, to be gathered up

like pig-corn, but you cannot gather it

yourselves. It would be like holding on

to air. Imagine each flower

pulling this ambrosia up, imagine it might,

like us, begin in darkness.

Geometry

> Essential,
with heaven nearly empty of

stars, with mountains still
rising from plains,

like music,

only it can't be heard.
> Before wax

we'd use it to build, carve
pine resin into cells,

fields within hollow trees,
hexagons wired into

our sleep. Vein

of amber, ploughed under by ice—
golden lozenge—

we are still inside.

Innocence

Scale the firs with augers,
bore holes for us to enter. Later still

cut the trees down, hollow
the trunks, lay them on the outskirts

in clearings. Once fear

subsides, place the hives outside
the kitchen, say a prayer, reach bare-
handed in, tear off a fistful.

Innocent as cattle,
we whispered, *bring us home,*

& you brought us home.

Amber

> To hover
> the imagined center, our tongues
> grew long to please it, licking
>
> the walls, a chamber built of scent,
>
> a moment followed by a lesser moment
> & a hunger to return. It couldn't
>
> last, resin
>
> flowed glacially from wounds in the bark,
> pinned us in our entering
> as the orchids opened wider. First,
>
> liquid, so we swam until we couldn't.
> Then it felt like sleep, the taste of nectar
>
> still inside us. Sometimes a lotus
>
> submerged with us. A million years
> went by. A hundred. Swarm of hoverfly,
> cockroach, assassin bug, all

trapped, suspended

in that moment of fullness, a
Pompeii, the mother

covering her child's head forever.

Melitopoles

When a warrior falls in battle,
beloved &

far from home, the melitopoles
sell their finest grade

to suspend his vanquished corpse in honey.
Thus his body will cease

to decay, will last the road
back. Seal him behind glass

& you could gaze upon

his unchanged face, tinted
amber, but glass
will not survive such portage. Even honey

cannot hold him forever,

his mouth forced open, shocked
eyes, every pore

now filled with sweetness.

Wax (Jesus)

Around it you built churches, vaulted

cathedrals, containers of
light. Wax transmogrified

into candle, candle
to his body, the wick his soul. Roses

surround the coffin, wax seals
the lid—thirty pounds burns constantly

under his bleeding hands, votives lit
by anyone with a coin.

Blind Huber (vii)

Endless parade, each thought un-

seen, one pushes onto the

next, replaces what

was, this chain whispered quiet—false

promise that, once under-

stood, it will end, transform to a moment

empty of thought. How

riddled, to sit in a garden, lungs

spooling the sky, the in

& the out, impossible

physics, each plea lined up,

each moment now measured,

weighed, a queen's limited frenzy

within a glass hive.

Paper Wasp

Because trees grew thick & demon-

full, you felled whole counties,
built walls against the night. Shack

gave way to city, city

to skyscraper, forest to plain. All this time
we've been building beside you,

in the eaves, in the trees your axes missed.
Look at the nest in the rafters,
look closely. Those red

streaks are fragments of your barn, paint
chewed to pulp. Everything

passes through us, transformed.

We chew the words off newspapers,
bodies off billboards,
even your clothespins, look at them closely—

each day thinner.

Xenophon's Soldiers

           In enemy country sometimes
you come upon a vessel

waiting in the road, a clay pot
brimming honey, your men weary.
Don't you wonder

why the village stands empty,
why those who fled

went empty-handed? Why would they leave
these jars behind? In the villages

near Trapezus, after sighting
the longed-for sea, ten thousand soldiers

lay as if dead, foolhardy scavengers

of poisonous honey, essence of rhododendron
& azalea. Three days they staggered thus,
those that could move, purging &

bent, unable to straighten,
& in those three days the battle

& all Persia, lost.

If you were fleeing your enemies,
wouldn't you load your body with food, strap
the jars to your back, no matter the weight? How else

to begin in a strange land? Remember

the ocean, how it carries a fisherman
year after year,

& one day simply pulls him under.

A man went to Mohammed and told him his brother had violent pains in his body, and the Prophet told him to give the sick man honey. He did as he was told, but soon came back to say his brother was no better. Mohammed answered, "Go back and give him more honey, for God speaks the truth, thy brother's body lies."

—Islamic folktale

Without

Without God you rip our bodies

apart, suck the honey
from our tails. With God you cannot trust

what even your own body tells you. In your book
we swarm a house, surround

a boy as he sleeps & lift him, only to set him down
unharmed. You saw us

lift your own son, hang his body
above your head—still

you need a prophet
to tell you what it means.

Pheromone

Sky electric after this midsummer

drought, but a day of rain
won't be enough. The clover won't return,
or the nights we slept the fields,

clinging to their petals. The keeper clips

the grass outside the hive,
& the old guard, full of venom,
prods us to attack. We stud his suit with stingers

until we hang dead from the netting,
until he becomes the word *enemy,* his arms

flailing. Jagged light

surrounds us, his son
waits in their cart, screams. The air
brightens. From this distance

he looks no bigger than a possum
as he mouths the word *father.*

Blind Huber (viii)

Each letter traced, an alphabet

dimly recalled—which

desk, what hand, to become

these words upon this sheet.

In primary school we got as far as "Hh,"

then the fever came,

sound it out: FEE, FEE, FEE—

the idea of an alphabet

begun, then the idea of a word, then the idea

itself, each bee

its cipher, a tiny letter hanging above the blackboard,

the parade of vowel &

consonant, its own contagious song.

Blind Huber (ix)

Scarlet fever, desperate hush—

as a child, it hurt more

to open my mouth, to ask for the cold

cloth,

than to be still. Unearthly still,

my body hung an inch

over my body, I could feel my heat rise.

To walk away I had to trade my eyes.

They ache at times still

when unexpectantly I come upon myself

sopping beneath a sheet.

Blind Huber (x)

Lilac-drunk, in the garden I will never

see, I wonder about

the queen, *her mystery.* Burnens

seizes the whole bees of both hives,

searching her out. *On the second*

of July, the weather being very

fine, numbers of males left,

& we set at liberty a young virgin. . . .

Mere sound, mere

sensation, I put my mouth to the hive, promise

their queen will return, though it's not

my charge. Each

morning, before the dew lifts, they cover my head—

jeweled statue. The queen

has the answer. *What are they doing now?* I ask.

Crawling over each other,

walking in circles, Burnens replies.

Wax Father

                        Each day
the son came for more, scraping comb

freshly laid, kneeling
apologetic. The father had

collapsed, the boy

wasn't ready, so he built a replica of the old man
in order to save him. When

the legs gave out he fashioned legs,
when the hands began to tremble
he fashioned hands,

& as the fever spread he made a head. At the

bedside, he studied the creases edging
his father's eyes, the bones pressing up from the cheeks,

the places the skull

turned inward. The lungs filled—
he built a torso. As he finished

each limb, each organ, he carried it to the church
& pinned it above the altar, until nearly

his entire body hung there.

Blind Huber (xi)

Empty box, handful of

bees—in a few days

a city, the exact city in a hundred

boxes. Take your dead

father's hand, as the shadow of the earth

blots out the sun. A telescope

pulls the planets closer

but aren't they close enough?

Statuary

Our dying does not fill the hive
with the stench

of dying, our bodies

powder, our bodies

the vessel & the vessel
empties.

Outside
the world hungers.

A cockroach, stung,
can be removed.

A careless child

forced a snail inside with a stick once.
We waxed over the orifice of its shell

sealing the creature in. And here,

the cellar of the comb,

                        a mouse,
        driven in by winter & lack.

        Its pawing woke us.

        Even twitching it reeked—worse
the moment it stopped.

                Now every day
      we crawl over it
             to pass outside,

the wax form of what was

           staring out, its airless sleep,

           the mouse we built
    to warn the rest from us.

Blind Huber (xii)

Thus transfixed, stare blank at one

immovable thing, ocean

or statue, fifty years thus, to see

if it moves. Burnens

covers the walls with prepressed

comb, factory-punched,

so we can live inside a hive,

my chair dead-center, beside my

queen. Chain after chain

of bodies, a fabric

above, lowering. Forty days

I sat, until the comb began

to press into my chest. Burnens

brought water at first, described their

labors, the tomb being built.

When he could no longer join me

I lived on what honey fell

to my lips. I wanted to see

if the hive moved,

& it did,

but not as much as I had hoped.

Burnens (i)

Never a question of staying, the end

never named. His words

move my hand, he speaks then

listens, the lid pried free, the brood-hum

now open to the sky.

They have a very nice sense of proportion

& the space required

for the movement of bodies. My ruler

measures the gap, I count each worker

& feed him the number. His words

move my hands, but I name

what is seen.

Unquiet

Eyeless he stares into a lamp, bedstraw
left crushed by his falling. They

linger, you say,

to ease your way through, you hold on
empty, white-

knuckled. Look at us now, without
body or box,

the son tangs a pot, begs us
to stay, the hive inside-

out, one mass, we lift,

like the soul as it exits the body,
except you can see us

& we are not quiet.

Q. Can bees be stopped from flying out in the snow in the winter and being lost?

A. No. If you close them up, they will fight themselves to death trying to get out of the hive, and if you put the colony in a building, you will find them all over a window or a door trying to get out. They become confused and are lost.

Q. I have one colony in which the bees have become very mean. How can I get rid of the queen? How can I find her?

A. There is only one sure way to eliminate the old queen and that is to find her and kill her.

Workers (foragers)

        After this seven-
month slumber, honey-stupored
& warm, we unfold our

wings, shake off

the hive, set out for buckwheat
& the low flowers of spring. We work
ourselves ragged, each day

going out, to come back heavy
with nectar & pollen. Seconds

collapse. In seven weeks we
fall, dried-out
husks, ravaged lace. Long

winter, we huddled
for warmth, our bodies the lamp,
honey the fuel

that kept us.

Blind Huber (xiii)

Some days

we turn the entrance to face the sun

some days

the queen is invisible one mile above, the queen,

unbeknownst to us, is

dead some days. Catholics pass clutching lilies in

the rain, workers

stagger the fields again, shocked by

each petal. It's Easter,

& not one of my visitors, learned men of

science, not one

will notice what's been taken, just a blind

man staring day after day into loud

air, propped before a vision

that can only fail. I point to the hive

& they stare at my hand.

Rain

                    Devil's paintbrush &
buttercup, three days of rain—
weeks

till blackberries. High summer
& no

nectar comes in. Pollen

washes off the lips of wildflowers, wastes
in mud. We are

murderous inside, eating our own
bodies, feeding off the winter

stores. Rot stench rises

from below, the
queen sends us out & we can't find

our way back, our wings
sodden. We crawl over

our sisters' bodies, lick mold

from their eyes, the hive
strangely silent, nothing to

occupy us. Even a daisy,

wretched housefly food, reeking
of rotting flesh—

I would wrap myself in it.

Mites

wander our bodies
like fog, with each breath

we breathe them in, they crawl inside
& hollow us
out. How to exist without

air, how to itch this deep
without tearing our flesh apart? All
is placed—the sun mid-

sky, meadow

above wetland—vigilant for what is
larger, warding off
vermin, drunken children,

& still
wrack enters us—contagion borne

on reassuring whispers.

Blind Huber (xiv)

Rare orchid, scant pollen—one could

almost number each drop,

heavy on the pistil, unable to reach

the floor. Summer done,

we move the hive into the green-

house, immense palace

of wax, an empire

poured into glass. The orchids ruin their sleep,

Burnens reports, they fight each other

for access. As a boy

other boys would take my arm & wag it,

force my hand to slap my own

face. Once

boys did this to each other, once I had

eyes in my head, I could see them

coming. Burnens raises a finger, one

by one to my lips, sticky with the

harvest. I name each

clover, stargazer, swamp flower.

Queen (failed)

                    Foulbrood,
the guards let them pass, I

smell them, but no alarm goes
out. Dank

corridors, weird silence, cold air
seeps in at night. Those

whose mouths adored me, soon
they will come, find me
in comb already full, the box

ripped open, the keeper's fingers
ranging over us. It's not

how I want to die. I want

my daughters' mouths on mine,

I want those who began in me
to suck the air out of me.

Workers (robbers)

Your queen stares blank & im-

mobile, her brood thick
with maggot

& mite. Wings &
scat litter the entrance, you

no longer carry your dead

away. The guards let us
pass, unaware who belongs & who

doesn't. Simply

part of the dismantling,
we bite

holes big enough for our
tongues

& drink each cell dry. Tonight
a possum

will reach a paw in & pull the
rest of you out.

You must be like
candy to them, cracked open, soft

bodies filled with honey.

Worker (lost)

Half-filled mugs of beer

sour in the sun, thick with
corpses. The busboy flings them

into the sewer. We

have scattered far, to city
& market, drunk on
cut watermelon. All I knew

was nectar,
the long tongues of wildflowers, an orchid

that swallowed me whole. Nothing
to return to, the queen dead, I
pressed against her until her eyes

hung empty. Afterwards,

the hive full of strangers,
none remained precisely me, none

I would die for.

Worker

Clover whispers, each
lavender globe. Nine

days in the fields, then our wings

are shot. Day three
I came upon an orchid, hidden in
a stand of pine—newly opened,

mouth wide,

a lacy white corridor, heaven
after the gloom of the hive. Stumbling
inside, the scent

pulled me deeper, not caring
if she closed on me forever.

Unfamiliar

What village, abandoned, what
farmland, a house you move toward,

how will it announce itself?

A light dim in the upper window,
a baby born open-eyed &

full of words? Years pass, look

around you. This garden,
overgrown. This glass box. There must be somewhere

else, but how
will you recognize it? Archangels

came down once, ordered bees to build
honeycomb in your mouth.
Where you found yourself

was home. What comes down now?

Burnens (ii)

Home was a jar, you could say,

& the jar shattered my hand, or

in my hand, or fell

from it. Whatever lived inside

powdered like

fingerprints, like a moth's wing.

It will never fly again. I wait at the

foxglove, the bloodrush of *yes*,

the spot of blue paint on the thorax, my

mark, two miles

distant. Who else

to make his words real? I wander room-to-

field, do his bidding. None of the

rooms connect, except by months, his room

a jar, clear as air.

Conjecture, text fragments and carbon dating suggest the rise of human civilization coinciding with the rise of bee-culture. Entire libraries, it is said, were devoted to the study of the honeybee, though most of these libraries were burnt and plundered, along with the rest of the ancient world, and the knowledge lost. François Huber, the 18th-century French beekeeper, blind since childhood as a result of scarlet fever, discovered, or rediscovered, much of what is now known about the honeybee. Some of what is known is that the majority of the hive is made up of workers, who assume a variety of roles for the maintenance of the hive. All workers are female: genetically, each worker is considered identical. Drones are males, somewhat graceless and clumsy, larger than any worker, yet comprising only a small percentage of the hive's overall inhabitants. They neither guard nor forage, their role being solely to impregnate the virgin queen, after which they die or are killed. Huber focused much of his energies on solving what he called *the queen's mystery*, specifically, how she becomes impregnated, *what transpires in the air.* After her initial nuptial flight as a virgin, the queen spends the rest of her life as a virtual slave, never leaving the darkness of the hive, continuously laying the eggs that will become the workers. The only difference between the queen and a worker is that the queen is raised on a diet of royal jelly, which transforms her, the composition of which is still somewhat mysterious. Only one queen at a time can exist in each hive. A queen can live for three or four years; a worker, depending upon the level of activity, lives from two months to a year. Burnens (his first name lost) was Huber's lifelong assistant. Their experiments spanned fifty years.

"Swarm": *Not two* is a line from what is considered the first Zen writing, according to M.P. Landis.

The epigraph that begins the second section is taken from the Orson Welles film.

"Melitopoles": The word translates as "honey merchants."

"Wax (Jesus)": Inspired by Edison's line: *I'll make electricity so cheap only rich men will be able to afford candles.*

"Paper Wasp": *When the Lord God created bees, the devil tried to make some, but his became wasps.* (German folklore, from Hilda Ransome, *The Sacred Bee*)

"Xenophon's Soldiers": Reference taken from Ransome, *The Sacred Bee.*

The epigraph that begins the third section is taken from Ransome, *The Sacred Bee.*

"Without": The book referred to is the Koran.

"Blind Huber *(x)*": Lines in italics are taken from Huber's letter to M. Bonnet, 1821.

"Wax Father": *He who offers a wax hand, the wound on his hand is healed; he who offers a wax foot, his foot becomes sound.* (Heine, 1810)

"Statuary": Image taken from Maurice Maeterlinck, *The Life of the Bee.*

"Burnens *(i)*": Lines in italics are Huber's.

The epigraphs that begin the final section are from *Dadant's Q&A on Beekeeping.*

debts

Atlanta Review: "Burnens (ii)," "Blind Huber (xiv)"

BOMB: "Queen (failed)," "Xenophon's Soldiers," "Melitopoles"

canary river: "Geometry," "Mites"

Columbia: A Journal of Literature and Art: "Blind Huber *(x)*," "Drones"

Emergency Almanac: "Blind Huber *(viii, xiii)*"

jubilat: "Blind Huber *(xii)*"

The Kenyon Review: "Twinned," "Workers (foragers)," "Queen"

New England Review: "Swarm," "Paper Wasp"

Open City: "Rain," "Workers (guards)"

The Paris Review: "Blind Huber *(ii, iii, iv, v)*," "Hive"

Perihelion: "Unfamiliar," "Worker"

Pleiades: "Without"

Ploughshares: "Burnens (i)"

Post Road: "Amber," "Statuary"

Provincetown Arts: "Workers (robbers)," "Wax Father"

Swerve: "Unquiet," "Blind Huber *(ix)*," "Innocence"

Tin House: "Pheromone," "Worker (lost)"

TriQuarterly: "Inside Nothing," "Workers (attendants)," "Blind Huber *(i)*"

"Virgin Queen" was included in *The Hand of the Poet* exhibit at the New York Public Library, curated by Rodney Phillips, 1997.

"Virgin Queen" also appeared in *Poets for the Next Millennium,* a limited edition chapbook, edited and printed by Michael Peich, published by Aurelius Press, 1997.

"Inside Nothing" was included in a *festschrift* honoring Stanley Kunitz on his 96th birthday, published by Sheep Meadow Press, 2001.

"Inside Nothing" also appeared in the online zine, bkyn.com.

"Inside Nothing" also appeared online in *Born* (www.bornmagazine.org) as a collaboration with the artist Pierrick Calvez.

Visual artist Amy Kaczur incorporated the poem "Hive" into a wall text piece entitled "The Erotic Life of the Apex Mellifera," May 2002, The University Gallery, University of California, Irvine.

I am indebted to all the above.

Also: the Fine Arts Work Center in Provincetown, the
MacDowell Colony, the Schoolhouse Center for Art and
Design, the College of Saint Benedict in Minnesota, the
Library of Congress and the Witter Bynner Foundation, the
John Simon Guggenheim Foundation, the Bread Loaf
Writers' Conference, the Amy Lowell Traveling Poetry
Fellowship, and New York University—
it all helped.

Many friends shared their knowledge and insights
with me over the years of writing these poems—
each precious.

Also, the following were essential in one way or another:
Mark Adams, Dorothy Antczak, Bob Bailey, David Brody,
Matt Brown, Peter Cameron, Michael Carroll,
Mark Conway, Caroline Crumpacker, Philip Glass,
Jared Handelsman, Edward Hirsch, Tony Hoagland,
Marie Howe, Nicholas Kahn/Richard Selesnick, Lily King,
Richard McCann, Sarah Messer, Linda Nagaoka,
Frances Richard, Paul Tasha, Fred Tomaselli,
Reetika Vazirani, Sarah Walker, Rebecca Woolf—
endless thanks.

NICK FLYNN's first book of poems, *Some Ether*, won the inaugural PEN/Joyce Osterweil Award, the Larry Levis Prize from Virginia Commonwealth University, and was a finalist for the *Los Angeles Times* Book Prize. He has received fellowships from the Guggenheim and the Witter Bynner Foundations, as well as the Amy Lowell Traveling Fellowship. For many years he worked as a ship's captain, as an electrician, as a caseworker with homeless adults, and as an educator, primarily for Columbia University's Writing Project, primarily in New York City public schools. These various occupations overlapped occasionally. Currently, he splits his time between Brooklyn, New York, and Provincetown, Massachusetts.

The text is set in Giovanni,
a typeface designed by Robert Slinbach.
Book design by Wendy Holdman.
Typesetting by Stanton Publication Services, Inc.,
Manufactured by Maple Vail Book Manufacturing
on acid-free paper.

Graywolf Press is a not-for-profit, independent press. The books we publish include poetry, literary fiction, and cultural criticism. We are less interested in best-sellers than in talented writers who display a freshness of voice coupled with a distinct vision. We believe these are the very qualities essential to shape a vital and diverse culture.

Thankfully, many of our readers feel the same way. They have shown this through their desire to buy books by Graywolf writers; they have told us this themselves through their e-mail notes and at author events; and they have reinforced their commitment by contributing financial support, in small amounts and in large amounts, and joining the "Friends of Graywolf."

If you enjoyed this book and wish to learn more about Graywolf Press, we invite you to ask your bookseller or librarian about further Graywolf titles; or to contact us for a free catalog; or to visit our award-winning web site that features information about our forthcoming books.

We would also like to invite you to consider joining the hundreds of individuals who are already "Friends of Graywolf" by contributing to our membership program. Individual donations of any size are significant to us: they tell us that you believe that the kind of publishing we do matters. Our web site gives you many more details about the benefits you will enjoy as a "Friend of Graywolf"; but if you do not have online access, we urge you to contact us for a copy of our membership brochure.

www.graywolfpress.org

Graywolf Press
2402 University Avenue, Suite 203
Saint Paul, MN 55114
Phone: (651) 641-0077
Fax: (651) 641-0036
E-mail: wolves@graywolfpress.org

Other Graywolf titles you might enjoy:

Some Ether by Nick Flynn
Bellocq's Ophelia by Natasha Trethewey
Deposition by Katie Ford
Too Bright to See & Alma by Linda Gregg
Donkey Gospel by Tony Hoagland